A Mark V (male) of B Battalion, near Hamel on 4th July 1918, the first occasion these tanks were used in action. It has a semaphore for communications fixed to the rear cab.

FIRST WORLD WAR TANKS

E. Bartholomew

Shire Publications Ltd

CONTENTS

Printed in Great Britain by PrintOnDemand-Worldwide.com, Peterborough, UK.

British Library Cataloguing in Publication Data available.

ACKNOWLEDGEMENTS
I would like to thank all my colleagues at the Tank Museum, particularly the Curator, George Forty, the librarian, David Fletcher, and the Photographer, Roland Groom. All photographs reproduced in this Book, including the cover illustration, are copyright of the Tank Museum.

COVER: Mark IV (Male) Tank 'Lodestar', 12th Battalion, Tank Corps, France 1918, by Tony Bryan.

BELOW: A Mark V (Male) heavy tank.

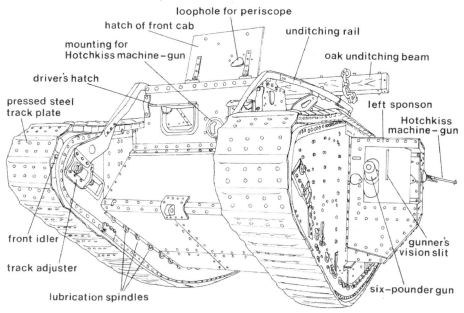

loophole for periscope
hatch of front cab
unditching rail
mounting for Hotchkiss machine-gun
oak unditching beam
driver's hatch
pressed steel track plate
left sponson
Hotchkiss machine-gun
front idler
gunner's vision slit
track adjuster
lubrication spindles
six-pounder gun

The Hornsby tractor, tested by the British War Office in 1910, was the first tracked vehicle in military service. Its original paraffin engine was later converted to run on petrol.

THE LANDSHIPS COMMITTEE

Fighting vehicles have been built since the first chariots, but for thousands of years they relied on men or animals for their propulsion. Chariots and siege engines fell into disuse as tactics became more sophisticated and although the invention of the steam engine provided a new source of power it inspired the creation of few military vehicles. When it did the advocates of steam war machines received little support. In Britain, for example, James Cowan's steam 'battle car' of 1855 was condemned as 'uncivilised'. Yet as technology increased its impact on warfare more nations adopted steam tractors for military transport. In the Boer War the British Army even used steam tractors as 'armoured road trains' for protection against Boer raiding parties. Petrol-engined vehicles proved more versatile, and by the beginning of the twentieth century engineers were adding guns and armour to commercial automobiles.

The development of these early armoured cars coincided with the first military use of tracked vehicles, in 1910, when the British War Office purchased four Hornsby tractors for haulage work. They performed well in trials but were not popular with some members of the General Staff, who complained that they were noisy, smelly and frightened horses. Two years later the Australian engineer de Mole met with a similar response when he showed the War Office his plans for an armoured tracked vehicle. Inventors of armoured vehicles in France and Austria had the same reception. In Britain interest in all tracked vehicles was so limited that in 1912 Hornsby and Sons sold their foreign patent rights to the American Holt Tractor Company.

When the First World War broke out in 1914 several armies used improvised armoured cars, but as the year drew to a close the conflict became increasingly defensive. Armoured cars were useless on battlefields dominated by trench systems and the infantry endured most of the fighting. As each offensive became increasingly wasteful in lives and resources armies began to search for new ways of crossing trenches, barbed wire and shell-torn ground.

In October 1914 a British Army officer, Lieutenant Colonel Ernest Swinton, suggested armouring the American Holt artillery tractor and using it to carry infantry or guns. His proposal was initially rejected, but in February 1915 a 'Landships Committee' was formed to examine plans for new armoured vehicles. The committee was composed of military engineers, Army officers and men from the Royal Naval Air Service (RNAS), who used armoured cars to defend their airfields in France. The naval influence was obvious in some of the early projects, such as Thomas Hetherington's land battleship. It was over 100 feet (30 m) long and armed with three twin-gun turrets. The committee

gave the Lincoln firm of William Foster and Company the contract to build a machine based on Hetherington's design. It was powered by a Foster-Daimler artillery tractor but was actually a giant wheel intended to crush barbed wire and other obstacles. The committee, however, halted work on the 'Big Wheel' when they realised that it was impracticable. William Tritton, Fosters' managing director, then used the artillery tractor as the basis of his 'Tritton Trench Crosser'. It could lay a girder bridge over small gaps and then recover it, but although one vehicle was completed it was rejected after trials in May 1915.

The Pedrail Transport Company of Fulham put the first proposals for a tracked vehicle before the committee. Their landship was designed to carry fifty infantrymen and ran on two single-track units. After lengthy delays an unarmoured version was built, but it was not resilient enough for trench warfare and was never used in action.

A British Army 75 horsepower petrol-engined Holt tractor at Kut in Mesopotamia. The tractor inspired armoured vehicle designs in several countries and its tracks were used on the first French, German and American tanks.

4

The Pedrail landship at Porton Down in Wiltshire. The Pedrail project was abandoned because of the machine's great weight and large turning circle, although it later took part in trials as a mobile flamethrower.

Pedrail was the only British company producing tracks, but it soon became clear that these were unsatisfactory. The Landships Committee therefore began to test American tractors. They began with the little Killen-Strait, which ran on a tricycle arrangement of three steel track units with wooden shoes. The Killen-Strait arrived in Britain in April 1915 and in demonstrations before Lloyd George and Churchill showed how tracked vehicles could overcome barbed wire and trench obstacles. The committee never intended to recommend the Killen-Strait for active service, but it was fitted with the body of a Delaunay-Belville armoured car to prove how more robust tractors could be adapted. This made the Killen-Strait the first tracked armoured vehicle.

The Killen-Strait tractor on trial at the headquarters of 20 Squadron RNAS at Wormwood Scrubs. The crewmen are Flight Commander Hetherington and Lieutenant Commander McGrath.

5

In July the committee tested two more American tractors, the Bullock 'Creeping Grip' machines. Two were linked together to form an articulated platform, but they were difficult to control and the coupling frequently broke. In another experiment a Bullock tractor was fitted with a framework of six wooden legs. These feet 'walked' alongside the machine and, in theory at least, stopped it from getting stuck in soft ground. The 'Elephant's Feet' project, like many others, was dropped after unsuccessful trials.

The Bullock tracks were used with much greater success on another machine, built by Fosters. After the rejection of his Trench Crosser William Tritton, partnered by Walter Wilson, built a new vehicle based on a specially lengthened set of Bullock tracks. Design work on this 'Number One Lincoln Machine' began on 11th August 1915 and by 14th September it was already running in trials. It had a box-like hull made of boiler plate and was powered by the 105 horsepower Daimler petrol engine used in the Foster tractors. Power was transferred through a two-speed gearbox and worm reduction gear to the rear sprockets, which drove the tracks. Tail wheels

aided steering and improved cross-country performance. It was not armed, but a dummy turret was fitted for the trials, weighted to simulate a two-pounder gun. In tests, however, the American-built tracks caused continual problems. The machine could only cross a 4 foot (1.2 m) trench, instead of the War Office specification of 5 feet (1.5 m), and the tracks often ran off their rollers. Realising that the Bullock tracks were inadequate, Wilson and Tritton decided to make their own. After several unsuccessful attempts they designed a cast-steel track-plate, which was riveted to hinged links. Guides engaged rails on the track frames and stopped the tracks working loose. The Number One Lincoln Machine was rebuilt using these tracks, with the frames lengthened to allow it to cross a 5 foot (1.5 m) gap. The new machine, called 'Little Willie', was the first armoured fighting vehicle with a purpose-built body and tracks — the first tank. The tracks developed for Little Willie were subsequently used on all the British tanks built during the First World War.

While Little Willie was still being built Tritton and Wilson were working on another design, capable of meeting new War Office requirements. Landships now

'Little Willie' with the new tracks designed by Wilson and Tritton. It took part in extensive trials, but soon after its completion was made obsolete by 'Mother' and was only used for driver training.

'Mother', the prototype for the British heavy tanks, on a test run in January 1916. It was made of boiler-plate and can be recognised by its rivets, which are more closely spaced than on production tanks.

had to be able to cross gaps 8 feet 6 inches (2.6 m) wide and climb obstacles 4 feet 6 inches (1.37 m) high. The new machine, called 'Big Willie', was radically different from the earlier vehicles, with a curved profile and tracks that went completely around its body. There was no room for a turret, so the two six-pounder guns were mounted on either side in half-turrets known as sponsons. Big Willie was made from boiler plate, riveted to a framework of angle iron. It had the same Daimler engine as Little Willie, but at 28 tons was twice as heavy. The extra weight would have put a great strain on its two-speed transmission so secondary gears were added to improve steering. The gears were operated by two of the eight-man crew who sat in the rear of the sponsons. The commander worked the brakes, which could also be used to turn the machine in an emergency. Tail wheels, like those on Little Willie, were an additional aid to steering.

Big Willie was completed in January 1916 and ran in trials only a month after Little Willie. It was underpowered and had a top speed of just 3 mph (5 km/h)

but could easily cross a 9 foot (2.7 m) gap. The politicians and military authorities were so impressed with its performance that in February the Ministry of Munitions ordered one hundred. In June the order was increased to 150. To preserve secrecy the production model was called the 'Tank Mark One' and the name 'tank' has been used ever since to describe tracked armoured fighting vehicles. Big Willie had various names, but in recognition of its role as the parent of all tanks it became known as 'Mother'.

Twenty-five Mark Is were built by Fosters, the rest by the Metropolitan Carriage, Wagon and Finance Company of Oldbury in Birmingham. Half of the tanks were built as 'males', virtually identical to Mother and armed with six-pounder guns and Hotchkiss machine-guns. A new version of the tank was also produced. The 'female' Mark I had modified sponsons, with heavy Vickers machine-guns instead of the six-pounders. A new unit, the Heavy Section of the Machine Gun Corps, was formed to work with the tanks and began training at Thetford, Bisley and Portsmouth.

The Mark I (male) C 19 'Clan Leslie' on the Somme, three days after the first tank action. The wire netting, intended to deflect grenades thrown on to the roof, was adopted only by C Company and was soon discarded.

THE TANK IN ACTION

In August 1916 the Heavy Section moved to France. The British General Staff wanted the tanks to be used as soon as possible, following the disastrous failure of the Somme offensive in July of that year. Sixty tanks of C and D Companies were assembled for a renewed attack which began near Flers on 15th September 1916. Mechanical failures meant that only forty-nine were ready by the day of the battle and of these just thirty-six reached their start positions on time.

The attack was a disappointment to those who had expected the tanks to lead a great breakthrough. They were introduced on difficult terrain and many of the crews had not completed their training. Some of the tanks were soon destroyed by artillery fire or abandoned after breakdowns, yet they achieved enough local successes to justify their designers' faith in them. Three tanks which attacked the village of Flers destroyed machine-gun posts and forced the defending Germans to retreat. One of them, D6, carried on to attack the next village of Guedecourt. 2 miles (3 km) to the east a C Company tank, *Creme de Menthe*, successfuly supported infantry in an assault on a German-occupied factory.

The crews faced conditions that soon became familiar to all the men who fought in tanks during the First World War. The Mark Is filled with the fumes of carbon monoxide from the engine and cordite from the guns. Their thin armour offered little protection, so molten lead, or 'splash', flew about inside whenever a tank was struck by bullets. To prevent injury crews were issued with face-masks of leather and chain-mail, but the heat from the engine was so intense that these were very uncomfortable and rarely used. The tanks had no suspension so the crewmen wore leather helmets to protect their heads, but these too were soon

ABOVE: *Corporal Seale and Gunner Tiffen manning the six-pounder gun of a Mark I in Palestine. The sights were rudimentary and aiming the gun was difficult because of the pitching and rolling movement of the tank.*

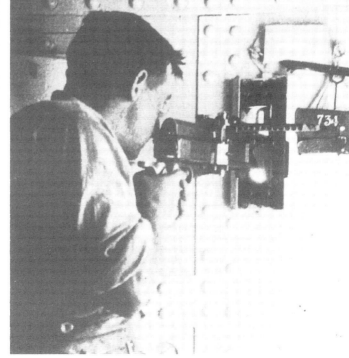

RIGHT: *A secondary gearsman firing a Hotchkiss machine-gun in a Mark I. Casualties among machine-gunners were high because the large aperture let in enemy fire. Later models of tank had a greatly improved ball and socket mounting for machine-guns.*

ABOVE: *Unloading fuel at Rollencourt 'tankodrome' in France. The heavy tanks used about 2 gallons of petrol for every mile (5.6 litres/km) they travelled.*

BELOW: *'The Perfect Lady', a Mark II (female) armed with Lewis guns, at Arras in April 1917. It has extra wide track shoes to improve grip and wooden undilching beams stored on the roof.*

discarded. They closely resembled German helmets and crews leaving damaged tanks had been mistakenly fired on by British troops. If a tank was hit escape was difficult as there were few hatches. There was always a great risk of fire, as fuel was fed to the engine by gravity and the petrol tanks were located in a vulnerable position high in the body.

The Mark Is were used in small numbers in the weeks that followed the first action and in November 1916 took part in a successful attack on the fortified village of Beaumont-Hamel. Tanks were not used again until the spring of 1917, but during the winter workshops and headquarters were established in France. The companies became battalions and recruitment increased. In Britain work on new designs continued, to meet a War Office requirement for one thousand tanks, with an extra hundred for training.

The training tanks were Mark IIs and IIIs, very similar to the Mark I and again produced in male and female form. They had a new hatch in the hull roof, a revised cab and, on most models, wider track shoes which gave a better grip. The new tanks had no tail wheels, because the crews of the Mark Is had complained that they were hazardous. Although effective in training, in France they often became stuck in mud and shell holes. Drivers noticed that without the wheels the tanks were easier to control, so the Mark I was the only tank fitted with them. They were removed from the remaining models in November 1916.

The Mark IIs, because they were only training tanks, did not have the usual face-hardened armour, but twenty-six were nevertheless sent to fight at Arras in April 1917. The three-week artillery bombardment which preceded their attack tore up the ground and gave the Germans time to prepare their defences. The tanks had some success but were held up by mud, snow and breakdowns and met increasing resistance as the battle wore on.

Failures like Arras were common in the tank's first year in action, because the General Staff consistently over-estimated the machine's abilities. They expected tanks to be able to cross virtually impassable ground and introduced the new Mark IV in appalling conditions, at Messines in June 1917.

The Mark IV kept the engine and transmission of the earlier tanks but

One of the fifty Mark IIs under construction. They were intended only as training tanks, but fought at Arras in April 1917.

11

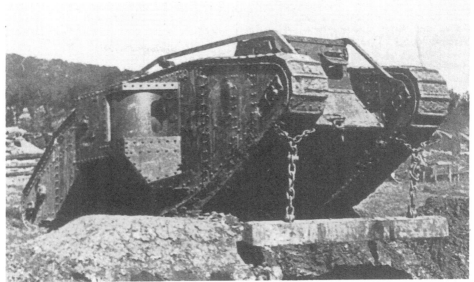

ABOVE: *A Mark IV (male) at the Tank Corps Central Workshops demonstrating the unditching drill. The beam, chained to the tracks, is about to be dragged underneath the tank, levering it out of the mud.*

BELOW: *A Mark IV (male) abandoned in a huge shell hole near Chateau Wood on the battlefield of Ypres. Whenever possible damaged tanks were stripped for spares — or souvenirs.*

'HMLS Kia Ora', a Mark I (female) of the Gaza tank detachment. Its Vickers guns in the large sponson are characteristic of the early female tanks.

incorporated several improvements made in the light of battlefield experience. It had armour 12 millimetres (½ inch) thick, proof against the German armour-piercing bullets which had penetrated the vulnerable Mark Is and IIs at Arras. To reduce the risk of fire the fuel tanks were armoured and moved outside, between the rear horns, with the petrol fed to the engine by a new 'Autovac' system. The Mark IV also had better ventilation and an exhaust — the first tanks had expelled fumes through a series of baffles on the hull roof.

The male tanks had a new version of the six-pounder, as the original guns were designed for naval use and the barrels proved to be too long for trench warfare. They were easily damaged if caught in buildings or in shell holes, so in the Mark IV they were replaced with shorter twenty-three calibre guns. The armament in the female tanks was also changed, with Lewis guns fitted in place of the Vickers guns. The Lewis guns, however, were unsuitable as their air cooling system sucked in dust and smoke, so they were soon exchanged for Hotchkiss guns. These lighter machine-guns could be mounted in a much smaller female sponson, allowing room for large escape hatches in the hull sides. The sponsons on both male and female tanks could also be

swung inwards for rail travel, to avoid collisions with bridges, tunnels or oncoming locomotives. When earlier tanks were transported by rail the sponsons were completely removed and had to be bolted back on before the tanks went into action. The sponsons weighed over 1½ tons and if the bolt holes had moved even slightly out of alignment mounting them could take several hours.

At Messines so many tanks were lost in the mud that in the summer of 1917 each Mark IV was given an unditching beam. It was fastened to rails which ran along the top of the hull and was chained to tracks if the tank became bogged down. The movement of the tracks pulled the beam underneath the tank, providing the grip for it to be able to climb out.

On 28th July 1917 the rapidly expanding tank battalions were reorganised into the Tank Corps. Three days later 230 Mark IVs were ready for the attack that began the Third Battle of Ypres. Intense rain and heavy shelling had turned the battlefield into an impassable bog and even the tanks' unditching beams proved useless. Only nineteen of the 136 tanks that took part in the first assault were still operational at the end of the day. The tanks fought at Ypres until October, but the mud severely restricted their impact on an offensive that eventually claimed

13

The Cambrai advance was halted after fierce fighting, in which two-thirds of the tanks were destroyed. This Mark IV (female) of G Battalion was knocked out in the 'Shooting Box' of Bourlon Wood.

over 200,000 British lives. Tanks received much of the blame for the failure at Ypres, and the future of the Tank Corps itself was uncertain.

While the tanks foundered in France and Belgium a small Tank Corps detachment fought the Turkish Army at Gaza in Palestine. Using eight old Mark Is they crossed gullies, dry river beds and rocky ground to attack Turkish positions. The detachment suffered heavy casualties in their first attack in April 1917, but the tanks were more successful in the Third Battle of Gaza in November. The Western Front, however, was considered far more important and it was in France that tanks were to play a decisive role.

As the Ypres offensive came to a halt the Tank Corps staff officers began planning a surprise attack on one of the strongest parts of the German Hindenburg Line. All the available tanks were to take part, using new tactics especially devised for the assault. To help cross the

'Merlin', a Gun Carrier with a six-inch (152 millimetre) howitzer, the wheels chained to its side. Gun Carriers were rarely used in their intended role and usually served as supply tanks.

A Mark IV salvage tank lifting part of the transmission from a tank at Central Workshops, Erin. Chinese labourers were responsible for much of the maintenance work.

wide German trenches the tanks were given fascines. These were large bundles of brushwood, weighing about 1½ tons and carried on top of the tanks, which were dropped into trenches and stopped the tanks from falling in.

By 20th November 1917 476 tanks had gathered along a 6 mile (10 km) front near the town of Cambrai. The attack began with only a brief artillery bombardment, allowing the tanks to move across firmer ground. Working closely with the British infantry they overwhelmed the German defenders and in one week had advanced an unprecedented 7 miles (11 km). Losses in the Tank Corps, however, were considerable and there was no reserve of tanks or infantry to continue the offensive. The Germans eventually recovered most of the ground they had lost, but Cambrai increased British confidence in the tank and speeded progress on new designs.

Tanks were not the only tracked fighting vehicles operating in France by this time. In June 1917 the first of forty-eight self-propelled guns arrived at the front.

The Gun Carrier Mark I was designed to transport either a 6 inch (152 mm) howitzer or a sixty-pounder gun, which could be winched on to an open platform at its front. It was built using components of the Mark I tank and had the same engine and transmission, housed in a compartment at the rear. The driver and brakesman sat in two armoured cabs on either side of the gun. The howitzer could be fired from the platform, so some gun carriers were used to shell German trenches, moving to new positions before they were spotted by enemy observers. Most of the machines, however, were used as supply carriers, as unarmed they could carry a 7 ton load. The Royal Engineers also built an excavator based on a Gun Carrier chassis, while two others were converted to serve as salvage tanks. The Tank Corps lost so many machines through mechanical difficulties that conventional tanks were also modified for salvage work. These were fitted with jibs, and occasionally winches, for recovering damaged tanks or for work at the Tank Corps Central Workshops.

ABOVE: *Mark IVs at a railhead before the battle of Cambrai. They are carrying the fascines used to cross wide trenches and their sponsons are swung inward for rail travel.*
BELOW: *A Mark IV (female) near Peronne. It has large escape hatches below the sponson and is armed with the Lewis guns adopted on early models of the tank. The undinching beam is stowed at the rear, chained to the rails on the roof.*

ABOVE: *A Mark IV (female) moving forward near Passchendaele in September 1917. Getting tanks to the front required careful planning. Often they were hidden in woods or camouflaged during the day and moved at night. The commander guided the tank by walking a short distance in front.*

BELOW: *The 'Tadpole Tail' lengthened the Mark IV and allowed it to cross trenches 12 feet (3.5 m) wide. Although supplies of the tails were shipped to France they were not strong enough for use in action.*

French Army FT 17s armed with 37 millimetre cannons. These Renaults include versions with both cast and riveted armour-plate turrets.

FRENCH AND GERMAN TANKS

FRENCH TANKS

While the Landships Committee worked in Britain the French, completely independently of their allies, were developing their own tanks. They began by testing wheeled agricultural tractors and road rollers and then conducted trials with tracked vehicles. In May 1915 the Schneider Company bought two American Holt tractors and demonstrated them to technical and artillery officers of the French army. Eugène Brillié, Schneider's Chief Engineer, was asked to design an armoured body for the 45 horsepower 'Baby Holt' and this machine was tested in December 1915. It was obvious that a larger vehicle was needed, so on 20th December Brillié was introduced to an artillery officer, Colonel Jean Baptiste Estienne, who had already produced tentative plans for an armoured Holt tractor. In the next six days Estienne and Brillié designed the first French tank,

the Schneider 'Char d'Assaut'. Two prototypes ran in trials in February 1915 and the Ministry of Armaments ordered four hundred.

The Schneider was a lengthened Holt chassis fitted with an armoured box. There was a girder at the front to cut through barbed wire and two tails at the rear to assist it in trench crossing. The tank was armed with a short 75 millimetre gun and two Hotchkiss machine-guns. It was powered by a 60 horsepower petrol engine and had a top speed of 5 mph (8 km/h). At 14 tons it weighed only half as much as the British tanks but it still had a crew of six men.

The Schneider aroused considerable industrial and inter-departmental jealousy and there was soon an 'official' tank to rival it. Known as the 'St Chamond' it was also based on lengthened Holt tracks and was armed with a 75 millimetre field gun and four machine-guns. The hull was much larger than the Schneider's with overhangs at the front and rear which seriously limited the tank's cross-country performance. A petrol-electric transmission made steering relatively easy, but contributed to the tank's greater weight of 29 tons. It was also delicate and unreliable. The tank had a nine man crew.

The Ministry of Armaments ordered four hundred St Chamonds, intending to use them with the Schneiders in a massive surprise attack. The first French tanks were not ready until 16th April 1917, when 132 Schneiders joined an attack at Chemin des Dames on the river Aisne. They were unable to cross German trenches except at specially prepared points and proved highly vulnerable to artillery fire. The Schneider's fuel tanks were located high in the body and exploded or burst into flames if the tank was hit. Seventy-six tanks were destroyed, mostly by fire, in this first attack, and over 170 crewmen killed or wounded.

The St Chamonds were first used three weeks later, when sixteen accompanied thirty-two Schneiders in an attack at Laffaux Mill. Nearly all of the cumbersome St Chamonds became stuck in German trenches and they repeated this performance in several later actions. The Schneider and St Chamond continued in service, but there were no new orders. By 1917 French tank production was concentrated on a very different design, a light, two-man tank built by Renault and known as the FT 17.

The FT 17 was a revolutionary vehicle, designed to operate in swarms and overcome opposition by sheer weight of numbers. It was the first tank to have its gun in a fully rotating turret and was armed with either an 8 millimetre machine-gun or 37 millimetre cannon. The tank weighed only 6 tons and was

A Schneider Char d'Assaut about to leave the factory. The 75 millimetre gun is mounted in the right side of the hull, with a Hotchkiss machine-gun behind it. The Schneider's fuel tanks were poorly protected and many were destroyed by fire or explosions.

powered by an uprated Renault car engine that gave a top speed of 6 mph (10 km/h). There were no concessions to the comfort of the crew and wherever possible Renault tried to reduce weight and costs. The large front idler was even made of wood.

The FT 17 was first used in the battle for the Fôret de Retz in May 1918 and took part in all the French tank actions that followed. Over three thousand Renaults had been built by the end of the war and the tank was still in service with the French Army in 1940. It was a very adaptable vehicle and the chassis was used as the basis of bridgelayers, mine-clearers, wireless tanks and self-propelled guns. FT 17s were also produced in the United States using American components and, although only ten were completed by the Armistice, eventually over a thousand of these 'Six-Ton Tanks' were built. After the war the FT 17 was widely exported and the design was also adopted by many nations producing their own tanks for the first time. In Italy the tank was developed as the Fiat 3000, while the USSR manufactured its versions, the KS and MS tanks.

An A7V chassis under test at the Daimler works at Marienfelde in Berlin. Without the armoured body the Holt tracks can be clearly seen. The A7V needed two drivers because of its complicated transmission.

GERMAN TANKS

German and Austrian engineers had designed armoured fighting vehicles before the First World War, but even after the onset of trench warfare they received little support from the military authorities. It took the British tank attack at Flers to prompt the German High Command into action and in October 1916 they formed a committee to co-ordinate plans for German armoured vehicles. The committee, known by its code-name of A7V, briefly resurrected a pre-war design, planning to build a 550-ton 'armoured land cruiser'. They soon aban-

doned this project and turned to road rollers and tractors, but these were unsuccessful in trials.

Joseph Vollmer, an engineer working for the committee, designed the first German tracked armoured vehicle. In early 1917 he fitted a tracked lorry, the Bremer Marien Wagen, with a steel body. Its tracks, however, like those on so many other prototype tanks, were ineffective on rough ground and only one was built.

These failures focused attention on the Holt tractor, which was manufactured under licence in Budapest. Vollmer de-

The A7Vs 'Hagen' and 'Wotan' in a French village in June 1918.

21

The 40 ton A7V/U copied some of the best features of the British heavy tanks. Its Holt-type tracks, however, tended to become clogged with mud and only this prototype was completed.

signed a lengthened version of the track unit and in April 1917 fitted a modified Holt chassis with a mock-up superstructure. The chassis was used for a prototype tank, the A7V Sturmpanzerwagen, which was tested a month later and then accepted for production. The box-like tank was armed with a 57 millimetre gun and six Maxim machine-guns. It was powered by two Daimler 100 horsepower engines and weighed 33 tons. It needed a crew of eighteen.

Production was slow and the tank did not see action until 21st March 1918. Five A7Vs, accompanied by captured British Mark IVs, overran British trenches at St Quentin, and all the defenders were either killed or captured. On 24th April about fifteen German tanks confronted British Mark IVs near Villers Bretonneux in the first ever combat between tanks. The A7Vs badly damaged two female tanks but were finally driven off by a male Mark IV.

The A7V, with armour 30 millimetres (1³⁄₁₆ inch) thick, was better protected than the British tanks and its two engines gave greater power and a top speed of 8 mph (12 km/h). Yet it had a high centre of gravity, which made it unstable on rough ground, and could cross only a 6 foot (1.82 m) gap. The Germans had little confidence in the A7V, and only about twenty were built. The majority of tanks used by the German Army were captured Mark IVs. These so impressed the High Command that they ordered a German tank based on the design, known as the A7V/U. It had all-round tracks but kept most of the components of the A7V. Only a prototype was completed.

The A7V was the only German-built tank that fought during the First World War. Work on the giant 100-ton K-Wagen and the LK series of light tanks was halted at the Armistice. The next German tank was the Panzer I of 1933, the first of a generation of armoured vehicles that completely changed land warfare.

ABOVE: *The A7V 'Schnuck' was abandoned near Bapaume on 31st August 1918 and captured in a later Allied advance. It was shipped to London for display but was scrapped after the war.*

BELOW: *The German LK II light tank was based on a converted car chassis. It was not used by the German Army, but the design was adopted in Sweden after the war.*

23

Six-cylinder, 150 horsepower Ricardo engines in the Central Stores at Erin in northern France. The Tank Corps needed vast workshops and stores to keep its vehicles running.

1918

The British attack at Cambrai had eventually failed because the heavy tanks had been unable to sustain their advance. In December 1917, therefore, the Ministry of Munitions authorised production of a new tank, designed to exploit such breakthroughs. This was the Medium A, which was very different from the heavy tanks, with a low track profile and built-up superstructure. It was powered by two 45 horsepower Tylor lorry engines, each of which drove a track through its own clutch and gearbox. This made the Medium A a very difficult tank to drive, as changing two sets of gears without stalling one of the engines required considerable skill. The fighting compartment was also cramped and badly ventilated and there were only three crewmen to operate four guns. At 8 mph (13 km/h), however, the tank was considered fast and became known as the 'Whippet'.

The Tank Corps had little opportunity to use the Whippets in their intended role, because they entered service as the Germans began their great spring offensive of 1918. Yet in their first battle, on the Somme in March 1918, twelve Whippets broke up an advance by about three hundred German infantrymen. They were in action again soon after the skirmish at Villers Bretonneux, but it was not until August 1918 that the Whippets realised their full potential.

The introduction of the Medium A gave the Tank Corps its 'breakthrough tank', but the arrival of the Mark V in July 1918 was even more welcome. The Mark V had an epicyclic gearbox which allowed it to be driven by just one man, and a purpose-built 150 horsepower Ricardo engine. Smoother gear changes, improved steering and greater power made the Mark V more manoeuvrable and more effective in action. Its 14 millimetre (9/16 inch) armour was also thicker than on previous British tanks. The tank kept the eight-man crew, the

A temporarily unarmed Medium A (Whippet) carrying extra supplies of petrol stowed on its armoured fuel tanks.

former gearsmen working as machine-gunners, and for greater firepower an extra machine-gun was mounted above the fuel tanks at the rear. Externally the tank differed only slightly from the Mark IV. It had a rear cab in the top of the hull, which improved the crew's vision and allowed them to release the unditching beam from inside the tank. It also had a new ventilation system, with louvres and a fan behind the sponsons. Four hundred Mark Vs were built, but the Tank Corps also used three hundred modified versions of the tank, known as the Mark V Star or V*.

The Mark V* was a standard Mark V, lengthened by the addition of 6 feet (1.82 m) of extra armour plates behind the sponsons. It could cross a trench 13 feet (3.96 m) wide without having to use fascines, which were bulky and difficult to recover once dropped. The tank could

The Mark V was 32 feet 5 inches (9.88 m) long. This female, about to leave the Metropolitan Works, is crewed by men of the Royal Naval Air Service, who tested all tanks before they left Britain.*

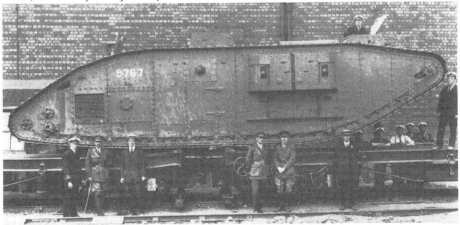

25

A Mark V** with a 20 foot (6 m) tank bridge carried on a hinged jib suspended in front of the tank.

carry twenty-five infantrymen in its spacious interior, but the heat and fumes usually made them too sick to fight, so the Mark V*s were rarely used as troop transporters.

The Mark V*s fought continually in the final months of the war, but the modification was not ideal. Steering was difficult, because of the long tracks, so a redesigned version, the Mark V**, was also produced. It was the same size as the Mark V* but there was less track in contact with the ground and the front horns rose a little more sharply to improve its climbing ability. The guns had

more sophisticated range-finding equipment and voice-pipes made internal communications easier. Twenty-five Mark V**s were built in November 1918, too late to see active service. After the war some were used by the Royal Engineers as experimental bridgelayers and mineclearers, the forerunners of the assault tanks used in the Normandy landings of 1944.

The Mark V* was the last British tank built during the First World War to see action, but during 1918 work continued on new designs. A Mark VI was built as a wooden mock-up but never entered pro-

The Holt 'Gas-Electric Tank' was the first American tank. Its petrol engine drove two electric motors, and it was steered by varying the current to each track.

The 9 ton 'Skeleton Tank' was relatively light, but it could cross wide trenches. The main structural members were iron pipes held together by standard plumbing fittings. It was armed with a 37 millimetre gun in a small turret.

The Ford 'Two-Man Tank' was armed with a machine-gun that had only a limited traverse. Ventilation was poor and the fighting compartment cramped and uncomfortable.

The prototype American Mark VIII on trials in 1918. The United States eventually built one hundred of these 'Internationals' and they were in service until 1932. At the beginning of the Second World War they were sent to Canada under the Lend-Lease scheme and used to train tank crews.

duction, while only three Mark VIIs were completed. For the great offensives planned for 1919 the Tank Corps expected to use a new tank, the Mark VIII. It was based on earlier British designs, but produced in conjunction with manufacturers in the United States.

American involvement with the Mark VIII began soon after the United States' entry into the war and followed trials with several experimental tanks. The first American tank was built by the Holt Tractor Company, whose vehicles played such an important part in tank development in other countries. Their 'Gas-Electric Tank' was similar to others based on the Holt tracks, with a box-like armoured body containing a 75 millimetre howitzer in the nose. It had a gasoline (petrol)-electric transmission to simplify steering, but only one of these tanks was completed. The Holt project was dropped in favour of tanks with all-round tracks, and a 'Steam Tank' and 'Skeleton Tank' were among several prototypes built. These American tank designs showed great inventiveness, but they were not practical enough to serve as fighting vehicles. Realising that tanks had to be produced without delay the United States Ordnance Department relied on French and British expertise and concentrated on manufacturing the Mark VIII and the Six-Ton Tank. They also decided to make a smaller version of the FT 17, known as the 'Two-Man Tank'. It was

built using American car components and was powered by two Model T Ford engines. 15,015 were ordered, but only fifteen completed.

The Mark VIII was the most advanced heavy tank of the First World War, larger and more powerful than all the earlier designs. It weighed 37 tons, but its American 300 horsepower Liberty engine still gave it a top speed of 6 mph (10 km/h). The Anglo-American Commission planned to build 1500 Mark VIIIs at a new factory in France, using American guns and transmissions and British hulls and tracks. Britain and the United States also agreed to produce their own, slightly modified versions of the tank. The British Mark VIII had two Ricardo engines mounted on a common crankcase, giving a combined output of 300 horsepower. All the Mark VIIIs were males, because they needed the six-pounder guns to combat German tanks.

The Mark VIIIs were expected to lead the armoured advance into Germany, but only five were completed before the Armistice. The end of the war also slowed production of a new range of medium tanks and a specialist supply carrier, the Mark IX.

The Mark IX was the last in the line of British tanks that began with Mother, although it was not really a fighting tank. It was designed to transport infantrymen or supplies and was armed with only two Hotchkiss machine-guns. The Mark IX

The Mark IX could carry thirty infantrymen or 10 tons of stores in its body. Extra supplies were transported on the roof or towed on sledges behind the tank.

The Medium B weighed 18 tons and with a top speed of only 6 mph (10 km/h) was slower than the first 'Whippet'. It did not see action during the war, but in 1919 fought with British tank detachments against the Russian Bolsheviks.

was ordered late in the war and only one reached France before November 1918, serving as an armoured ambulance. In Britain the prototype was fitted with flotation tanks and took part in amphibious trials on a reservoir in Hendon.

To support the Mark VIIIs and IXs there were new Whippets. For improved cross-country performance Wilson's Medium B was shaped like the heavy tanks, with the crew compartment and 100 horsepower Ricardo engine in the hull. Forty-five of the machine-gun armed Medium Bs were built, but they were cramped, underpowered and difficult to maintain. The Medium C 'Hornet', designed by Tritton, was a far better tank. It had the more powerful 150 horsepower Ricardo engine, and included several features suggested by tank

crews. There were voice-pipes for communications and a rotating cupola for the commander. Forty-eight production models, all females, were completed, but they were never used in combat. The third tank, the Medium D, represented a radical departure from earlier designs. It had a 240 horsepower engine and despite weighing 20 tons could reach a top speed of 20 mph (32 km/h). Flexible tracks gave it a smooth ride over rough ground.

The mediums were designed to play a major role in an armoured attack planned for 1919. In the event none were used, because the German Army collapsed following the tank offensive that began with the battle of Amiens.

On 8th August 1918 over four hundred tanks were concentrated near Amiens for a massive attack that smashed through

A blazing Mark V (male) at Bray in August 1918. In the last four months of the war the Tank Corps lost over a third of its men and more than eight hundred tanks were sent to Erin for salvage or repair.

LEFT: *The Medium D was the most sophisticated First World War tank. Steered by bowing the flexible 'snake' tracks, it had a top speed of 20 mph (32 km/h). Only four prototypes were completed before the war ended.*
RIGHT: *The Allied advance ended with the occupation of Germany. This Mark V, in Cologne in May 1919, is a hermaphrodite with both male and female sponsons. It needed the six-pounder to combat German tanks.*

the German defences. Medium As and Austin armoured cars advanced beyond the heavy tanks, causing panic among the retreating Germans. Amiens was followed by a succession of attacks that broke German morale within three months. They also stretched the Tank Corps to its limits. Losses were so severe that only eight Whippets were available for the final tank battle of the war, at Mormal on 5th November 1918. Nevertheless, the tanks had played a vital part in the Allied victory and the German Supreme Commander, General Ludendorff, acknowledged this. He called 8th August, the date when the offensive began, 'the black day'.

CONCLUSION

Britain produced the best tanks during the First World War and by the Armistice had built more than 2800. The British tanks owed their success to Wilson and Tritton's far-sighted 'Mother' and the thorough trials carried out by the Landships Committee in 1915 and 1916. The heavy tanks were the ideal shape for conditions on the Western Front and their trench crossing and climbing ability has hardly been bettered. Yet, apart from the small detachments used in the Russian Civil War, the British heavy tanks never fought again after 1918. They had proved that 'impregnable' defensive systems could be defeated and had made trench warfare largely redundant. Freed from its constrictions the British designs of the 1920s were far more mobile than their predecessors, with low tracks and guns in rotating turrets. By contrast, in France, the failure of the St Chamond and Schneider led to an emphasis on tanks with all-round tracks that persisted into the Second World War. It was a policy that resulted in tanks with an ill-conceived layout and poor fighting performance.

The German Army probably learned most from the use of tanks in the First World War. They had suffered because they had originally regarded tanks with contempt and were slow in responding with their own, inadequate, A7V. Yet the Germans did not forget their tank defeats of 1918. When they rearmed in the 1930s they led the world in creating an armoured force that exploited the power of tanks to the full.

30

FURTHER READING

Several books on this subject, some of which are listed below, were published in the years immediately after the First World War. Copies of them may be found in libraries. Information about early tanks may also be found in military journals of the same period.

Browne, D. G. *The Tank In Action*. William Blackwood, 1920.
Chamberlain, Peter, and Ellis, Chris. *Tanks of World War I — British and German*. Arms and Armour Press, 1969.
Crow, Duncan (editor). *Armoured Fighting Vehicles of World War One*. Profile Publications, 1970.
Fletcher, David. *Landships — British Tanks in the First World War*. Her Majesty's Stationery Office, 1984.
Fuller, J. F. C. *Tanks in the Great War 1914-1918*. John Murray, 1920.
Liddell Hart, B. H. *The Tanks — The History of the Royal Tank Regiment and its Predecessors* (Volume I 1914-1939). Cassell, 1959.
Stern, Albert. *Tanks 1914-1918 — The Log Book of a Pioneer*. Hodder and Stoughton, 1919.
White, B. T. *Tanks and Other Armoured Fighting Vehicles 1900-1918*. Blandford Press, 1970.
Williams-Ellis, Major C. and A. *The Tank Corps*. Country Life Ltd, 1919.

A reminder of the first tank action — German prisoners breaking up a Mark I towards the end of the war. It still has the Russian inscription 'With Care to Petrograd' adopted in September 1916 to confuse German spies. Today only one Mark I survives.

PLACES TO VISIT

Few First World War vehicles remain, but there are still small numbers of tanks in collections throughout the world.

GREAT BRITAIN

Imperial War Museum, Lambeth Road, London SE1 6HZ. Telephone 01-735 8922. (Contains a Mark V (male).)

National Army Museum, Royal Hospital Road, London SW3 4HT. Telephone: 01-730 0717. (Contains a specially commissioned diorama of the tank attack at Cambrai.)

The Tank Museum, Bovington Camp, near Wareham, Dorset BH20 6JG. Telephone: Wareham (0929) 462721 extension 463 or 329. (The museum contains the most important collection of First World War tanks in the world. There are nine First World War tanks, including 'Little Willie', the only surviving Mark I, a prototype Renault FT 17, a Medium A that fought at Amiens and a Mark IV which is the oldest working tank in the world. The collection also includes the 1909 Hornsby tractor.)

The city of Lincoln has a Mark IV (female) on long loan from the Tank Museum. At Ashford in Kent a Mark IV (female) donated to the town in recognition of money raised from war bond sales is on display in the town centre.

AUSTRALIA

Australian War Memorial, Top of Anzac Parade, Reid, PO Box 345, Canberra City, ACT 2601. (Contains a Mark IV (female) and a Renault FT 17.)

Queensland Museum, Gregory Terrace, Fortitude Valley, Brisbane, Queensland 4006. (Contains 'Mephisto', the sole surviving A7V.)

BELGIUM

Musée Royale de l'Armée, Avenue de Tervuren, Parc du Cinquantenaire, 1040 Brussels. (Contains a Mark IV (male) and a Medium A.)

CANADA

Base Borden Military Museums, Canadian Forces Base, Worthington Park, Borden, Ontario L0M 1C0. (A 'Six-Ton Tank' and a Medium A are on display.)

FINLAND

Parola Tank Museum, Parolannummi, 13700 Hattula. (Among the exhibits is a Renault FT 17 delivered to the Finnish Army in 1919.)

FRANCE

Musée des Blindes, Saumur, Maine-et-Loire. (There are examples of machine-gun and cannon-armed FT 17s.)

UNITED STATES OF AMERICA

US Army Ordnance Museum, c/o US Army Ordnance Center and School, Aberdeen Proving Ground, Maryland 21040. (Tanks on display include the Holt Gas-Electric Tank, a Mark VIII, a Medium A, a Schneider, a St Chamond and other First World War tanks.)

Patton Museum of Cavalry and Armor, Old Ironsides Avenue, Fort Knox, Kentucky 40121. (A British Mark V* (male) and a Ford Two-Man Tank are displayed.)

USSR

At Archangel a British Mark V (female), a legacy of the Russian Civil War, is displayed in a square in the city